Abigail to Zipporah

BIBLE WOMEN IN RHYMES AND QUESTIONS

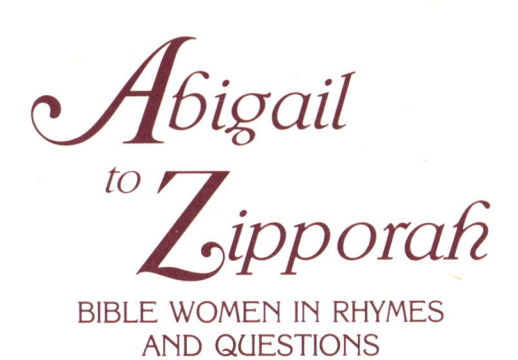

Rosemary Frantz

Abingdon Press

ABIGAIL TO ZIPPORAH:
Bible Women in Rhymes and Questions

Copyright © 1987 by Abingdon Press

All rights reserved.
No part of this work may be reproduced or transmitted in any form or by any means, electronic or mechanical, including photocopying and recording, or by any information storage or retrieval system, except as may be expressly permitted by the 1976 Copyright Act or in writing from the publisher. Requests for permission should be addressed in writing to Abingdon Press, 201 8th Avenue South, Nashville, TN 37202.

Frantz, Rosemary, 1929–
Abigail to Zipporah.

Summary: Rhymes about Old and New Testament women, each followed by a related question which can be answered by referring to a cited Scripture reference.
1. Women in the Bible—Miscellanea—Juvenile literature.
2. Bible games and puzzles—Juvenile literature. [1. Women in the Bible—Miscellanea. 2. Bible games and puzzles]
I. Title. II. Title: Bible women in rhymes and questions.
BS575.F73   1987   220.9'2'088042   87-999
ISBN 0-687-00031-9 (pbk.)

Scripture quotations marked NIV are from the Holy Bible, New International Version. Copyright © 1973, 1978, International Bible Society. Used by permission of Zondervan Bible Publishers.

MANUFACTURED BY THE PARTHENON PRESS AT
NASHVILLE, TENNESSEE, UNITED STATES OF AMERICA

Introduction

Abigail to Zipporah is a collection of rhymes about Old and New Testament women, arranged alphabetically. Each rhyme is followed by a question about the woman, which can be answered by looking up the Scripture reference given. *Abigail to Zipporah* is an educational tool, a learning activity, and an entertaining game!

Designed for use in the home, Christian schools, and Sunday schools, *Abigail to Zipporah* encourages children to read the Bible and helps them learn to use Scripture references. Through these rhymes and questions, children, parents, and teachers will meet many fascinating women. (Note: For a few letters, only one name or none can be found in either Testament. For letters without proper names, a significant word has been chosen for the rhyme and question.)

A Word to Parents and Teachers

In working through this activity booklet, children will look up fifty-one separate Scriptures. The spelling of proper names conforms to the New International Version of the Bible, which was used to prepare these rhymes. While any Bible version may be used, the answers to certain questions will be clearer if the NIV is used. Show the children the table of contents in their Bibles, where they can look up the beginning pages of the less familiar books. Talk about the division of each book into chapters and verses, then try some of the rhymes and questions.

You'll soon see many ways this activity booklet can be used. For instance, you can make a game of finding the answers: "Who can find the answer first?" You might also develop reading skills by asking children to read the verse or verses that answer the question. You can go back through the rhymes and questions again later, finding out more about the woman named by reading some of the verses before and after the reference. Was she a mother, a daughter, a wife, or a sister? Was she a believer in the one God? What kind of woman was she?

After using the activity for a while, make a game of answering the questions without reference to the Scripture verse!

A Word to the Young Reader

The heroines in many of our books seem never to do anything wrong. Our Bible is a very unusual book in that its heroes and heroines are not perfect! Our Lord wants us to know that even when we make a mistake, He still loves us and can use us for His purpose.

In this book, you will meet women who chose God's way and some who did not. Some of the names will seem strange because they are from another language and are not heard in our country. Try saying their names aloud.

To find the answers to the questions about each woman, look up the rhyme's Scripture verse in your Bible. Enjoy your search from *A* to *Z!*

The Lord God said, "It is not good for the man to be alone. I will make a helper suitable for him." . . . So the Lord God caused the man to fall into a deep sleep; and while he was sleeping, he took one of the man's ribs and closed up the place with flesh. Then the Lord God made a woman from the rib he had taken out of the man, and he brought her to the man.

Genesis 2:18, 21-22 NIV

ABIGAIL was really pretty.
She was smart and also witty.

What was the name of Abigail's nasty husband?
1 Samuel 25:3

NABAL

ANNA was a very old lady
When God let her see His Holy Baby.

How old was Anna? *84*
Luke 2:25-38

BATHSHEBA was a beautiful queen.
Her son, Solomon,
Became a very wise king.

Who was the father of Bathsheba's son?
1 Kings 2:1

_____ DAVID _____

BERNICE came to the audience hall
To see and hear a man named Paul.

What was the name of the king who was with Bernice?
Acts 25:13, 22-24

CLAUDIA helped the apostle Paul
Work and work and give his all.

Who, besides Claudia, sent greetings?
2 Timothy 4:19-21

COZBI led an Israelite man astray.
She made him worship her god one day.

What was Cozbi's father named?
Numbers 25:15

DEBORAH and Barak sang a great song.
There was peace in the land forty years long.

Why had there been war in Deborah's land?
Judges 5:1, 8, 31

DORCAS was sick, then she died.
All her friends cried and cried.

What did Peter say to Dorcas?
Acts 9:39-40

ELIZABETH was very old.
Her husband, Zechariah, was very bold.

Who was the son of Elizabeth and Zechariah?
Luke 1:13

John

ESTHER was a lovely young queen.
She knew Haman, who was grouchy and mean.

To whom did Esther tell the story of the evil Haman?
Esther 7:1-6

FAITH is believing what you cannot see.
It is believing so truly that it comes to be.

Who will live by faith?
Habakkuk 2:4

What did Jesus say to the people who followed Him?
Matthew 8:10

GOMER was an unfaithful wife.
She was unfaithful almost all her life.

Who was Gomer's husband?
Hosea 1:2-3

_____ Piblaim _____

Today, GRACE* is often a lady's name.
It is also the gift God wants us to claim.

To whom does God give grace?
Proverbs 3:34
Ephesians 4:7

*Note: Some Bible versions use the word "favor" instead of "grace."

HANNAH was Samuel's mother.
He had two sisters and three brothers.

What did Hannah tell her husband? *About Samuel*
1 Samuel 1:22

As soon as the child is weaned, I will bring him, that he may appear in the presence of the Lord, & abide there forever.

HERODIAS, a woman who was very cruel,
Thought John the Baptist was a fool.

What did Herodias tell her daughter to ask for?
Mark 6:21-24

With God there is nothing IMPOSSIBLE,
Though sometimes we act as if life's all trouble.

What makes it possible to please God?
Hebrews 11:6

We know very little about ISCAH.
She did have a sister named Milcah.

Who was the father of Iscah?
Genesis 11:29

JEMIMAH's name means "little dove."
I bet she was full of peace and love.

Who was Jemimah's father?

Job 42:12-14

JOANNA traveled with Jesus and His friends,
And often their clothes she would mend.

Besides Joanna, who else traveled with Jesus?

Luke 8:1-3

KETURAH married a man named Abraham.
Three of their sons
Were Zimran, Jokshan, and Medan.

Who were Keturah's other three sons?
Genesis 25:1-2

KEZIAH and Keren Happuch
Were two more daughters
Job loved very much.

What did Keziah look like?
Job 42:14-15

LEAH had six sons and a daughter. Jacob was their famous father.

What was Leah's daughter named?
Genesis 30:20-21

LOIS was Timothy's grandmother. We don't know his grandfather.

Who was Lois' mother?
2 Timothy 1:5

MARTHA was a very hard worker.
Often Jesus came to visit her.

What did Martha do when she heard
Jesus was coming?

John 11:20

she went & met him outside

MIRIAM had two famous brothers.
Aaron was one, Moses the other.

What did Miriam and the women do once
the Israelites were safe?

Exodus 15:20

NAOMI's husband and two sons died.
She was very, very sad inside.

When Naomi left Moab, who went with her?
Ruth 1:22

(handwritten: Ruth her daughter-in-law)

Our NEIGHBOR can be
　Our friend next door,
Or someone down the road
　Who is hungry and poor.

How should we treat our neighbor?
Galatians 5:14

To be willing to OBEY
　Dad and Mom every day,
Is the very best way
　To be happy at play.

Who is pleased when we obey our parents?
Colossians 3:20

ORPAH decided to stay at her mother's home.
She did not leave with Naomi to roam.

What did Orpah do when Naomi left?
Ruth 1:14

The wife was PRISCILLA.
The husband was Aquila.

What group of people met at the home of Aquila and Priscilla?

1 Corinthians 16:19

PUAH didn't obey the king.
For him she wouldn't do a thing.

What did Puah tell the king?

Exodus 1:15-19

QUENCH means to put things out.
We quench happiness when we pout.

What cannot be quenched with water?
Song of Solomon 8:6-7

What is holy that we should not quench?
1 Thessalonians 5:19

Jabob loved RACHEL, not Leah,
Not Leah, Maria, or Dorothea.

What were Rachel and Leah like?
Genesis 29:16-18

RHODA was so happy and sunny;
She did something really funny.

What did Rhoda do?
Acts 12:13-14

SAPPHIRA lied,
Then she died.

What did Peter ask Sapphira?
Acts 5:1-2, 8

Tell me whether you sold the land for much

SARAH made her very best bread.
She made it from a recipe
She kept in her head.

Who told Sarah to make the bread?
Genesis 18:6   *Abraham*

TAMAR was a beautiful woman.
Her father's name was Absalom.

How many brothers did Tamar have?
2 Samuel 14:27

TRYPHENA lived in Rome—
That city was her home.

What was Tryphena's sister named?
Romans 16:12

When we UNDERSTAND someone,
Knowing them is enjoyable and fun.

Who promised us understanding?
Psalm 119:169

Whose peace passes all understanding?
Philippians 4:7

The king ordered Queen VASHTI
　To come before him at his party.
When she told him no,
　He thought she was a smarty.

How did the king behave when Vashti said no?
Esther 1:11-12

Let us sing and rejoice
When we hear God's VOICE.

What else should we do when we hear God's voice?
Revelation 3:20

There are two kinds of WISDOM—
   Between them we choose.
With one you can win,
   With the other you lose.

Who gives us winning wisdom?
Proverbs 2:6

What is foolishness in God's sight?
1 Corinthians 3:19

When a mother EXPLAINS,
Sometimes she entertains,
Sometimes she causes pains.

What was Samson's riddle?
Judges 14:14-15

Why is it hard to explain things to some people?
Hebrews 5:11

YIELD, produce, give, and bear,
These words mean hard work
And lots of care.

Why will the land yield a good harvest?
Leviticus 26:3-5

What does a fig tree *not* yield?
James 3:11-12

ZIBIAH taught her son what was right.
He was a good king in God's sight.

What was Zibiah's son named?

2 Kings 12:1-2

ZIPPORAH was the woman Moses married.
When Moses went back to Egypt,
At home she tarried.

How did Zipporah meet Moses?

Exodus 2:16-21